Suggest Parad

t Paradise

Mary Burritt
Christiansen
Poetry Series

Mary Burritt Christiansen Poetry Series

Hilda Raz, Series Editor

The Mary Burritt Christiansen Poetry Series publishes two to four books a year that engage and give voice to the realities of living, working, and experiencing the West and the Border as places and as metaphors. The purpose of the series is to expand access to, and the audience for, quality poetry, both single volumes and anthologies, that can be used for general reading as well as in classrooms.

Also available in the Mary Burritt Christiansen Poetry Series:

Victory Garden: Poems by Glenna Luschei

The Gospel of Wildflowers and Weeds: Poems by Orlando Ricardo Menes

Reflections through the Convex Mirror of Time / Reflexiones tras el Espejo Convexo del Tiempo: Poems in Remembrance of the Spanish Civil War / Poemas en Recuerdo de la Guerra Civil Española by Tony Mares

The Loneliest Girl: Poems by Kate Gale

Walking Uphill at Noon: Poems by Jon Kelly Yenser

origin story: poems by Gary Jackson

Nowhere: Poems by Katie Schmid

Ancestral Demon of a Grieving Bride: Poems by Sy Hoahwah

The Definition of Empty: Poems by Bill O'Neill

Feel Puma: Poems by Ray Gonzalez

For additional titles in the Mary Burritt Christiansen Poetry Series, please visit unmpress.com.

Suggest

Paradise

Poems

RAY GONZALEZ

Suggest Paradise

University of New Mexico Press   *Albuquerque*

Library of Congress LCCN: 2022945911

Founded in 1889, the University of New Mexico sits on the traditional homelands of the Pueblo of Sandia. The original peoples of New Mexico—Pueblo, Navajo, and Apache—since time immemorial have deep connections to the land and have made significant contributions to the broader community statewide. We honor the land itself and those who remain stewards of this land throughout the generations and also acknowledge our committed relationship to Indigenous peoples. We gratefully recognize our history.

Cover illustration by Isaac Morris

Designed by Isaac Morris

Composed in Helvetica Neue, Sabon 11 | 14

CONTENTS

Part One

Part 1

The Trees

The trees want to touch each other.
They wish to get closer because of

the state of the world, must become
one tree before the landscape changes.

When their mysterious leaves float
to the ground, a man sitting under

one tree extends a hand and touches
the brittle falling.

The trees gather their limbs, and
branches spread beyond the man's sight.

The act of catching a handful of leaves
is too late to transform anything.

The sunlight reflects what he can't see,
until more leaves come down.

Their darkness becomes one tree filled
with shapes of other trees that release

their shadows when the last leaves fall.
The man was never there to see this.

Offering Birds

In the middle of my afternoon nap,
my two-year-old granddaughter Scarlet
runs into the bedroom to offer me
a bird, her imagination carrying
one in her tiny palm.

"Papa," she says, "here is a bird."
She comes to my side of the bed
and places it in my hand.
I am surprised and say, "Thank you,"
as she runs out of the room.

I lie back, then again, "Papa!"
She runs in with a closed fist,
and I reach out with one hand.
"'Nother bird," she says quietly,
and I take it, put my hand to
my heart and hold back tears
of blessing and joy.

She does this two more times,
the four birds nestled in my heart
as she hurries out of the room,
wings beating, and I wonder how
large the flock will get before
I am fully awake.

Two Hands at San Elizario

When I climbed there, the two hands
waited palms up, the white paint
fading long ago, the exact location
kept from me for generations,
until I read it in a poem I did not
write, the rock waiting to be found
without reaching out to receive.

As I stood there, the two hands
were open in sunlight, the fragrant
leaves on the tree shading the hands
and folding them, until the town
below disappeared.

When I descended, the two hands
were still there, each foothold
hiding where I had been, the rock
untouched for others to find,
fingers extended because one hand
signaled when I closed my fists.

Gift for a Believer

This body is made of mesquite and prickly pear,
thorns blazing in the night sky from a rare

fall of rain, arms and legs extended to interrupt
the water, this body so thick with green it can't

be seen without an explorer's map that drives
the history of the canyons away, the trail of ribs

and bare hips covering the true story of conquest
and the driven hands lost in the dusty wind.

This body carries itself cold and hushed,
mountains blended into the head of the stars

that fall onto the back, a spinal fire following
the believer into the energy of sand, feet burning

to signal the body has walked into a cave
filled with clay from the thumbs, the knees,

and the eyes that closed the touching rain.

The Train

I

The distant train came out of
the black cloud and blew its

whistle five miles south of the house,
waking me each night at 2:00 a.m.

My interrupted dream followed
the tracks along the border where

the railroad stretched but never gained,
my life as a twelve-year-old allowed

by the romance of a train I could
never catch or see, daydreams of

leaving the desert becoming nights
of lying awake, waiting for the sound

to drop its cargo and blow free,
the empty cars now filled with

fleeing men, San Antonio bound,
their desperation filling my sleep

with black engines and cries drowned
by the smoke of the horn.

II

The child of the train is ticketed
all the way to the coast where

dead grandmothers wait to teach
them how to keep tracking the lost
who never made it home.

Each child of the train arrives
in black smoke, disembarks alone,
the sleeping cars too far to reach,
the engine having lost its roar,
a dark town unknown because
no one there dreams of the railroad.

III

Desert sunlight changed
to a railroad union town

where my mother was born.
I have not been there

since I was a boy because
the train blasting through

the heat of the past did
not cease in Arizona.

We drove through the town
on the way to California

because she wanted to show
me the house, but the train

derailed in a dream where
remaining homes were torn

down, smoke from the black
engine hiding the dead,

turning each body into
a monument surrounded by

tall saguaros that were
the things that bled.

IV

Coal in the heart,
black animals in the lungs,
the man shoveling more
at the engine that burns
lies into ashes of family lore.

No one knows the history
of the desert rails.
No one can forgive
the foreman who left
his loved ones behind.

V

The railroad bridge woke me,
passenger cars flying into
the river that reached the stars,
train wheels crossing high over
the baptismal water where I was
held by a mother and father
who refused to get off the train
because there was something
to prove, sprinkled drops on
my forehead as black as the bridge.

VI

The distant train came out
of the white cloud near
Fort Thomas, Arizona,
burning to get there on time
because only one train
can be lost in a lifetime,
its children riding and
staring at mountains,
the whistle blasting its way
over the long curve of
a smokeless sunrise,
leaving the empty
railroad station behind.

The Cane

Jim Harrison used a cane to
find birds on his walk, the stick
of a one-eyed man who was as
sharp as a hawk, though his
spine failed and challenged him
to make his way up there.

Maybe, that is the problem—
Harrison disrupted sparrows,
wrens, and hawks scrambling
to get away from his tapping—
the bird lover climbing up the hill,
his cane holding him up, the legs
of the man shuffling toward the sun
so he can listen to the music
of the king.

Suggest Paradise

Suggest paradise and close your eyes.
Cottonwood Springs is left behind.
What flies out of there leaves a stain
in the struggling heart.
Twilight burns outside of El Paso.
How often do you recognize
the Spanish conquest?

Suggest purity and find the notes
carved in the old cottonwood
between La Mesilla and Rincon.
It is the alphabet from the map
to the broken branches.

Messages on your forehead gleam
with moonlight stolen from your
father before he entered the gates.
Do not listen, simply hear.
Carlos Malinquez became someone
else when the branches grew through
his chest on the crucifix.
Suggest paradise so we all can bleed.

Photographs of the Dead

They were passed on to me
so I could gaze at family I never
knew, railroad days in Arizona portraying
my grandfather Jose as a hero with
his cowboy hat and overalls,
his railroad crew joining him in several
portraits of the working dead, 1930.
Many of the photos were taken in
cemeteries, the grave markers and
crosses next to Jose and my grandmother
Julia, even his brothers who stand by
the tombstones, smiling into the camera

as the desert blazes above the graves.
In one photo, my mother at age thirteen stands
with her sister and brothers around Jose's
grave, 1941, the hot El Paso sun vaporizing
their grief when they step off the train from
Arizona that left many dead behind,
their forty-four-year-old father turning to dust,
dead aunts and uncles stepping behind
Jose's headstone to squint into the light.

The Silence of Fernando Pessoa

I am here, and I want to listen.
There are sounds that could be named.
There are windows stained by the hands of fame.

I stare at dandelions in the grass.
They come from a world that insists.
I can walk without saying a word and

will not go home by way of the sea because
the mute desert is closer and I have vanished.
My feet are two owls fleeing the earth,

their wings disappearing each time I walk,
the sensation of a great wind not stirring
the dandelions because they grow too short.

I am here, and someone will close the book
for me because to speak would become
a sentence waiting to be written.

The Error of Sleep

I must be a scar.
Glad window and
the domination of the period.
Escarpment.
My wheel used to spell "blood."
I must be a scar.

Look of expertise.
Placement overrides shadow.
Pattern commits to motion.
Footprint.
Proud concrete.
I must be a scar.

You were the paradise of form.
A watt of beauty.
Torn ear sounds like torn ear.
The path leads across the field.
I must be a scar on that road.
Anything the gods want to send.

Lack of attention to Greek myth.
Obedience derives from trying too hard.
The child is asleep in the back.
Midair wail.
The background mist.
A system noted for its ability to transcend.

I must be a scar.
The shovel and the fat eye.
Taboos.
Explicit Rex.
Frank O'Hara.
He doesn't come out to play.

He is not a scar.
The period one week after the comma.
The comma one week after the book says,
"I must be a scar."
You were never a scar.
You were a sentence.

Mornings

Let me study the outline of a leaf
embedded in mortar and brick.

The last one I traced brought me
good luck with pen and ink.

I will prove silence is composed
of decisions and tender smiles.

These are my letters that contain
what I have never written.

Whatever deities believe in me,
I pass by the carcass of a crow.

It blesses me with its ugliness,
and I ask for the bread cure

because there is a city
where I can go and sing,

the honeysuckle dripping
the same water as the sea.

Broken Boy Soldier

I wake in a sandbox of toy soldiers,
plastic and metal ones from my childhood.
They lie everywhere—Yankee soldiers from
the Civil War, doughboys from World War I,
and knights from who knows when.
Some of the soldiers lie in groups.
A few World War II men hide in the dirt
with their feet up in the air.
The bravest are still alive.
I pull a handful of my favorites from
the dirt and put them in a plastic case,
where I keep all of my soldiers.

I sit up when I realize who is missing,
my legs crushing the US cavalry.
I am alert because the lone soldier I had
from the Iraq war is missing—my nephew
is not in this large sandbox in the backyard
where I leave my plastic dead every night,
going inside the house at dinnertime,
abandoning battles because I know
how the fighting will turn out.

One collectable Army soldier from
the early twenty-first century is missing.
I can't find my nephew who volunteered
to join the service a few years ago.
He is gone, and I kneel in the dirt to plan
where to deploy soldiers to find him.
I dig a tunnel, certain my nephew was buried
the last time I set up a huge battle.
Confederates attacked, and the Knights of
the Round Table held them off so
Special Forces dudes could get away.

The news from overseas convinces me
to choose one of my best soldiers to be him.
I am playing with my toy soldiers in this
sandbox because I am a grown man who
has awoken to count the soldiers.

Before I disrupt battles with rocks,
I must bring my nephew back from
the dead so I can display him again.
It is time to stop the war and go to
my room, stop pretending and play
some other child's game.

As it grows darker, my mother calls
to me to come inside.
She has the news about her grandson.
I yell that I am coming and stand to
shake the dirt off my knees.
By tomorrow, I will dig new trenches
and tunnels, add the new army tank
I finished gluing together yesterday.

Conversion

Who plucked one eye out of the sparrow and lived to tell it.
Who forgot the beautiful skull and found a bag of pomegranates.
Who entered the doorway to the wrong house and lay in a stranger's bed.
Who kissed the glimmering jewels and grew a sequence of flowers.
Who feared the breath of anger and gave blankets to the poor.
Who learned the secret of heaven and sang all the way home.
Who fell in the rain gutter and heard the cry of the goat.
Who coated amphibians with the light of the moon.

Who stared at the headlights and kept a diary each night.
Who identified the wisteria and annihilated the giant in the storybook.
Who hungered after the soul and was devoted to tiny stones on the floor.
Who suffered the fever of children and described a tropical fish in a poem.
Who withdrew from the ocean after whispering into a seashell.
Who testified in favor of nostalgia and was faithful to his wife.
Who adjusted the acoustics and left his faith inside the museum.

Who ate in the monastery and stared at a tree that looked like God.
Who was told to be wiser than the scars on his hands.
Who understood imagination before drawing a face with three eyes.
Who escaped as a starfish and was rescued from the communion line.
Who regained strength inside an isolated room.
Who blew out candles as men gathered in the square.

Serpent Words

In states of ecstasy after bloodletting, Mayan nobility call the vision serpent. This serpent rises from the burning bloody paper of creation, and from its mouth emerges a deity that knows the words. A bare foot stamps the burning paper with blood, emergence given one sentence of seven words to complete the burning. If this sentence is done before everything turns to ashes, the wish will be granted. The seven words can't be revealed. If the bloody paper disappears before the seven words are formed, two serpent heads will appear. The bloody paper must be translated by the one who has been bitten.

In Mayan calendars, the fifth day is *snake* and is reserved for collecting the pattern of seven words and eating the parchment to regurgitate it. When the speaker of the seven words throws up, the mass is wrapped in snakeskin from the dreaded fer-de-lance, the snake that gives no warning as it strikes, the speaker of the seven words shaking long enough to wrap the gift in the snakeskin of the sacrificed, revenge complete when the seven words force the snake to belch humans from its mouth—a warrior, a god, and a skeleton.

Their bitten hands are fused to the bloody paper that confiscated the skeletal hands. The serpent is a conduit of water. The second is the snake's mouth being a cave and the third is that the serpent is the sky. Seven words keeps raining into a clay jar hidden in a cave that has never known the sun. To bring the sun into this erases the bloodstains from the burning paper.

T-Shirt Shop on Santa Fe Street

I almost bought a T-shirt with
Pancho Villa's face on it,

the bandido pointing a finger,
"Ese, Gringo! I want you!"

His huge moustache and sombrero
would be perfect for Minnesota.

They didn't have my size so I almost
bought the famous Che Guevara face,

revolution alive and well on the border,
but I had worn that years ago.

I found La Virgen de Guadalupe
on a green T-shirt, perfect size,

but I hesitated because I couldn't
wear her on my chest, candles of

recent mourning holding me back.
I bought a soccer T-shirt, the sport

big down there, this team claiming
a rhinoceros for a mascot, the image

rather small, though its horn raged
across my stomach as I tried it on,

wished Pancho Villa had been there
to warn me the animal that rages

is the creature that chooses us
when other T-shirt sizes are wrong.

Stack of Tortillas

I was told to stop writing
about my grandmother's tortillas
I grew up on and can't taste again,
though the dream serves me
dozens of hot tortillas off her
stove as I sit at the kitchen
table and dig into my bowl of
frijoles fresh out of the pot.

I wake in her kitchen, a boy
sweating from biting jalapeños
and tearing pieces of tortilla,
the soft texture of paradise
too delicious to give me any
sign of the future where a cold
stove in darkness is where
eternity is served its meal.

The Language of Sunlight, 1956

I gave up speaking my native Spanish
when I was five years old.
My grandmother Julia raised me,
and I heard Spanish all day.
My memories of Saint Mary's
Catholic Church in downtown El Paso
are filled with the cruelty of the nuns.

They beat kids on the head with yardsticks.
If you got caught chewing gum, it would
get stuck to your chin.
The nuns' job was to make sure no one spoke
Spanish in the classroom, the cafeteria,
or the playground. Spanish was against
the rules and punishable by a beating

with the paddle, the whacking sounds and cries
of the kids followed by the screeching nuns,
"English only! Do you hear me?
English only!" Whack! Hard blows on
your rear and off to your desk.
I never got caught because I didn't know English.
When I ran into my cousin Benny, who went
to school there, we whispered in Spanish.

My kindergarten teacher was Sister Irene,
a tall nun who resembled the stork
in the picture books she read to us.
She loved to move students around the room.
We were assigned a seat, but after we found
where to sit she would scramble the order again.

We studied the eight basic colors.
Sister Irene divided the class into groups,
four of us per color with poster cards
and the name of the color on each.
I understood what she wanted us to do
as we sat quietly in our new desks,
mine now closest to the hallway door.

The sister told us to stand when it was
our color's turn. When she held green,
the four kids assigned that one rose
and repeated the color.
We started this game late in the day,
some of us having to catch buses
and get home miles from downtown.
The final bell would ring in five minutes.
Sister Irene told us to sit quietly
and held up the orange card.
Four kids stood by their desks and repeated
the word "orange."
"Very good, Samuel. Yes, Leticia."
She held green and the group stood, "Green."
Anticipating my turn, I gripped the edge of
my desk and stretched to look at the cards.
The red card had not been held up.

Three colors left, including mine.
Sister Irene raised the blue card, and I stood
with the four kids in the blue group.
Laughter broke out, jeers growing louder!
I was frozen and could not sit down.
Sister Irene's menacing look scared me.
"No, Ramon! You are in the red group! Red!"
She yanked the card from her lap and waved it at me.
When the laughter stopped, she said,
"Ramon, you stay after school until you
learn your colors. Sit down."

Dizzy, I fell into my seat.
I did not know what
"stay after school" meant,
though I knew it was bad.

The sister held up the yellow card after the blue.
I watched the four kids get up through my tears.
I whispered, "Yellow." The final card was mine,
and I stood and croaked the word "red" with my group.
Suddenly, the bell rang!
Students grabbed bags and headed for the door.
The sister was surrounded by excited kids
and did not see me leap out of the room.
I ran across the schoolyard in terror,
found my cousin, and we boarded the bus.
It pulled away without any nuns after me.
The next day nothing happened, because
the sister forgot she told me to stay after school.
As I made it to the final bell, I pulled out my
box of eight crayons and recited them to myself.
Later, I turned to Benny on the bus.
He stared at me as I said, "Red, blue, green,
purple, brown, black, yellow, and orange."
Those were my first words in English.

One Pinto Bean

One pinto bean is all I have left
from the stereotype I gave up decades
ago when I tired of my brown shadow.
The pinto is brown and sits on my bookshelf.
I had it glazed, wanting to preserve the last bean
so I could meditate upon it when I missed the old
days of stuffing myself with pots of frijoles, stacks
of tortillas, and jalapeño peppers.

The bean shines with a lacquered glow as
it leans against a tiny pedestal I made for it.
If I get closer and stare at the bean, it will
move a fraction of an inch until it resembles
my bald head. I wish I had words to describe
how my bean is a miniature recreation of myself.
I want to deny this because I believe in
the freedom to separate myself from my past,

though preserving my bean is something
I could regret because it is shrinking, its skin
wrinkling despite the lacquer I sprayed.
It is turning dark like the moles on my skin.
I see myself on the dots that mark my throat
and arms as I search for my face in the bean.
I grab it off the shelf and walk into
the kitchen, wondering if the vegetable
soup on the stove could use a touch of
something I have not tasted in years.

Night in the Border Town

The old sadness is drunk and painted black.
Each street corner glows then lights
the door into the Chinese opium den,
underground passages never discovered
in the history books that burned.

The old tin roof of the whorehouse is
hammered in three languages as the escaping
horses mount the clouds with no way back.
The pickup truck hits the blind gambler
and he keeps walking, feathers of the raven
found on the road the next day.

The night becomes an archive of the living,
the carefully quiet, and the movement in
the trees where someone leans forward
without looking back, his search for

the drowning saint in the river changed to
a rescue of survivors from the radio station
hit by lightning, fires put out in time to move
to the tiny music coming out of the darkness
because, in this town, nobody dies in a flash.

Fear of Dying

My graduating student says the manuscript
for her first book is about the fear of dying.

She announces this as she reads poems
to a small audience that listens quietly.

I am startled because I have seen the poems
and discussed them with her without thinking

they are about the fear of dying, the window
striking the light and becoming something

we encounter over and over again.
I am surprised I overlooked it

and wonder if I missed it because
what I find in poems is what I have lived

in my lines about my grandmother
flying into my bedroom window on

the morning she passed away,
how I saw her for an instant, then

woke up knowing she was gone.
When a poet admits the fear of dying,

the silence between words contains the river
she last crossed when no one was watching,

going there to find out if what is being
sought is the same as what is written,

wondering if the lines that fill her pages
are going to stop the moment

the window shuts and the light
stays in the room and changes it.

The Coins

Why should I explain how I learned
to walk again? Is it the trinkets in
a canoe or the hieroglyphics on a turnip?
Last night the moon dropped its clothes
in the street where the trees cast a near light.

I learned to walk on dirt, not water.
My adobe geometry was left unsolved
when I ran to the dust with drowning hands,
improving my faith in brick alleys with sparks
on the road.

I handed myself a Roman coin.
Their attraction to light is mistaken for
my sanctuary, where a beetle is carved
on the clock I blink at each morning.

My hands understand there is nothing to read
because I wrote about markings in
the history of hatred, the word "canyon"
spelled backward because the first tree
became sacred in Greek history and made

me adopt the hare, more coins, and the pig.
They were taboo in ancient Britain before
the beetle floated in water and the poet
and the priest clashed before each took
turns washing his hands.

Solar Eclipse Totality, 2017

Millions of Americans drove across
states to watch something that lasted
for two and a half minutes.
Some wept and one couple got married
at the moment of totality.
Their marriage was eclipsed.
One woman in Wisconsin died in a car
wreck coming home from her solar trip.
Her car was eclipsed.

Nuclear bombs waited on board Guam
bombers, naval destroyers, and submarines.
Even on the other side of the planet,
the bombs were eclipsed.
In the Midwest, cows lay down in fields.
At that moment, their fields were eclipsed.
Shadows of tiny crescent moons appeared
on sidewalks and under trees.
Tiny faces in those shadows were eclipsed.

No Robert E. Lee statues were pulled down
that afternoon, because Robert E. Lee was eclipsed.
Giraffes in the Nashville zoo galloped in
circles at the moment of totality.
That circle was eclipsed.
A woman in Oregon silk-screened solar
T-shirts and sold eighteen thousand by herself.
Her hard work and money were eclipsed.

At the start, Trump looked up without
protective glasses and went blind.
His blindness was eclipsed.
In the year 610, Muhammad's youngest son
died on the day of a total eclipse.

His father was eclipsed.
Birds in trees went silent.
Silence was eclipsed.

Looking skyward, the "oohs" and "ahs" of
the crowd were mistaken for peace.
Peace was eclipsed.
Ku Klux Klan sheets hanging on
clotheslines went black.
Their blackness was eclipsed.
In Kentucky, a woman was killed
when a car swerved into people
waiting for the solar event.
Their waiting was eclipsed.

Two rare albino pigeons were spotted
in Minnesota, the pair caught by
the camera waiting high up in a tree.
Their whiteness was eclipsed.
A headline in the *Boston Globe* read,
"The Eclipse Will Pass Overwhelmingly
Over Trump Country."
The news was eclipsed.

Millions of Americans saw the same thing
in the sky, for a change, and were in awe.
Their sameness was eclipsed when the awe
disappeared on the way home.
Border walls in the Southwest were not
climbed that afternoon, arrests down
in a twenty-four-hour period.
The border wall was eclipsed.

Part Two

Pueblo Dancers, Santo Domingo, New Mexico, 2004

I have no choice as the circle begins to spin,
drums confusing those who are not from here.
There is no definition for the feathers streaking
inside this ritual, what I steal dropped in the dirt

as they move even faster, adobe walls washed
in a brown film where I can't breathe,
tourists standing frozen in time, voices,
rattles, and drums castigating the earth.

The God I know created the angry world.
These dancers are not gods from another but
men moving in a circle stricken by light and time
where the corn thrives through swaying arms

and legs that wait for the brown rain.
They steal something from me, then return it
as I witness what I can't understand.
I take something from them and don't

want to give it back when I step away,
tourists staring and sweating in the sun,
and I keep my secret nameless and broken.

Quietly Look Back

A Mexican man sells tacos
on a street corner, my father
missing for fifty years, the Holy
Ghost trapped in the old
confessional I first entered
as a kid, a trail of piss
running down my leg.

A Mexican man climbs over
a prison wall and gets away,
distant city lights going out,
UFOs crossing the desert night,
my pet pigeon found dead in
the trash can the day after
my first confession.

Living in silence, photographs of
a dead revolutionary soldier are
studied when it is prophesized
that Mexico has a revolution in
the tenth year of each new century.

A Mexican man with a tattoo of
Jesus runs along the Rio Grande,
shouting to his son to climb out
of the river before it is too late,
my high school hero scoring
the winning touchdown in the city

championship game, his head
decapitated in a drunken car
wreck three years later and two
years before Martin Luther King

is shot dead. Living in silence,
the stereotyped image of a fat
obandid with a sombrero is afraid

to cross the border north these days
because it is too late to change history
and no one studies the rebellion anymore,
the year 2010 arriving with drug cartels
as the new stereotype.

A Mexican man is impaled
on a cross, the drug deal gone
bad, the deepest hole ever dug
by machines in the New Mexico
desert ready to accept enormous
containers of radioactive waste,

my father betraying my mother
at a roadside motel, the hooker
a woman he would later marry
before celebrating an American
border without guilt.

The Women

One dark night in Juárez,
I walked past an old woman
with no legs, her stumps
hidden under a black skirt
mounted on a flat board
with tiny wheels.

The beggar reached out for coins
and grabbed my bottle instead.
There were fireworks in the night
sky and bullets in the border museum.

Vivian, my first girlfriend in high school,
was the 1970 ROTC beauty queen
before she rebelled and protested
the Vietnam War all by herself.

I was still in shock that she chose me
to be with her after she broke up
with her old boyfriend, though
I did not know what to do when
she got close after we saw Sly &

the Family Stone on our first date,
my hippie girlfriend and the beggar
woman rising out of the river to
sing me my favorite songs.

The Silence of Aime Cesaire

I have my sleepwalker hands.
I am awake, and my pearl diver

hands have grabbed me by
the throat because I refuse

the epidemic of drums.
The pounding is loud with

History, and my spirit cheese is
an insult to many men.

They smell what I have to say,
but my hands shrivel with

the blow of omens.
I cannot stare at silence

without knees in the sand.
When I let go, tom-toms laugh.

It is too far across the land,
and my stormy spume is

a blind peacock magical and cool.
Who said I am afraid?

There is an anger that leaves
a bouquet in my mouth.

The Hidden Notebook

I hid my first writing notebook
in 1964, at the age of twelve when
poems started appearing to me.
After rhyming words and coming
up with odd hippie images,
I shoved the dime-store journals
under my bed and acted as if
nothing were there, composing
rhymes in secret imitation of
the Beatles, though I came up
with my own words in silence,
jotting them down in the middle
of the night, my flashlight beaming

on the white pages before placing
them carefully inside a shoebox,
several months of pocket-sized
spirals hidden because I realized,
early on, that my poetry was knotted
in secret, the fist of emotion
hitting me in private because that
is the way it had to be, making sure
my sleeping parents in their bedroom
were not disturbed, my imagination
staying by itself for years because

I was constantly scolded for not
going outside to play baseball with
other boys, the hidden notebooks
filling with lines and stanzas for
the future when I could slide
the notebook out and open it to
write something about the sun,
first feelings set on the small page
about finding dusty roads out of there.

The Sparrows, 1978

*Once, at El Paso toward evening, I saw
and heard ten thousand sparrows who
had come in from the desert to roost.
They filled the trees in a small park and
men ran from them, their ears ringing.*

× William Carlos Williams, 1954

The memory of dead sparrows arises
from the desire to be there, again,
on the July afternoon when the rainstorm
came close to being a hurricane in the desert.
It rolled through a black sky, a rumbling
wall of water crossing from Mexico to hit
El Paso with seven inches of rain in three hours.
It crashed into the cottonwoods in front
of my house, tearing the green branches off
in a splintering roar of water and wind
that hit like steel pellets.

Hundreds of sparrows made their nests
and perched in those trees each evening.
The birds landed in clusters and filled
the branches with a loud chirping.
The gray cottonwoods turned brown
with the mass of birds that filled
the trees with singing.
The mystery was the way the birds
stopped chirping at once!

This happened every evening as
the sun burned orange in the western
sky over the Rio Grande.
The birds would suddenly be quiet,

at once, on a single note. One second,
the loud noise would drown others in
the area, the next instant stopping
together as if on cue.
The unexpected silence forced itself
through the grove of cottonwoods.
Then, they resumed their song,
thousands of them together.

I witnessed this a few minutes before
the storm from Mexico swept across
the river, smashing against the house,
breaking many trees and carrying branches
and chunks of earth in rushing streams
that flooded the yard.
I stood on the porch as rain
pounded the roof,
soaking me because I did not want
to go back into the house.

The afternoon sky turned black
and purple, growing deeper as
the storm moved north.
Bushes and trees bent low to the ground,
the wind shrieking higher as the bristling
rain shot leaves off the trees, a sea of
mud and grass rising quickly.
I tried to see if there were any birds
in the trees, hundreds of dead
sparrows floating around me.
Unable to fly, they were swept off
the trees and scattered across
the yard that was a small lake,

sparrows floating and spinning away
in a circle of mud and splintered branches.
The water rose as the fist of the storm

passed slowly toward the mountains.
The porch flooded, and I stood shin
deep in the mud until a loud flash
of lightning drove me into the house.

By the next morning the rooms
were flooded, mud filling the place
with an earthy odor.
As the morning sun focused
on the dead birds, the smell
spread across the yard.
In the afternoon I went outside to
take a break from cleaning.
Birds littered the surrounding
trunks of broken cottonwoods.
The brown and yellow sparrows
looked like tiny toy birds,
bloated bodies floating delicately
among the uprooted landscape.
The water was not going anywhere,
the lake holding flocks of the drowned.

I counted over five hundred birds near
the porch and estimated a couple of
thousand spread throughout the yard.
I waited two more days for the water
to slowly recede, then buried thousands
of sparrows in a huge arroyo carved
out of the yard by the rain.
I gathered shovelfuls all day.
By evening, I cleared much of the yard.
I piled the bodies in the arroyo, filled it
with mud, and covered it.

Walking back to the house, I noticed
the sound for the first time since
the storm, the trees full of sparrows,
more birds than before.
They returned to fill the air.
I stood on the porch, listened to
the chirping, and waited until they
quieted at once, on one note.
I went into the house when they started
singing together, again.

The Death of Walt Whitman

March 26, 1892, Camden, New Jersey

They are killing Walt Whitman tonight.
One thousand mourners pass through
his house in three hours, and they keep
crushing the poems on the floor.
Copies of *The Deathbed Edition of
Leaves of Grass* are scattered and
stepped on to make room.
They are washing Walt's body tonight.

No one notices his words are on the floor.
The mud and earth have spelled the way,
his house slowly sinking into the ground
because they are destroying him
in search of poetry, the white spirit.
They grant Walt pneumonia this evening,
his tuberculosis blessing the river with troops
parading by his oak coffin, which is
barely visible under the mound of flowers.

Poems of love grow out of his hair,
the crowds believing it because they
want the old, bearded face to open
its eyes before they stop looking.
They are taking Walt apart tonight.
Someone will steal his heart, and
America is a thief for his soul.
They are killing Walt Whitman tonight.

Ancient Aliens

The TV presents nerds who call
themselves "ancient alien theorists."
They insist we came from little green
men thousands of years ago and
did not evolve from apes.
Their proof is buried in my collection
of books on the Aztec and Mayan world.
The theorists claim the strange symbols
are not native but were created by
aliens who changed our history.

When I study those pages, I am
learning the little-green-men tongue.
I was taught about apes in school
to hide ideas implanted in our
brains eons ago when the mother ship
landed and legions of creatures got
out and painted graffiti on temples,
clay jars, and statues of gods.
So much for Hernán Cortés.
He didn't burn Mexico City down.
The ancient aliens did, because they
did not approve of the Aztec pyramids.

When my wife was in high school,
a small UFO chased her through the low
canyons near the Montana ranch
where she grew up.
To this day, she describes the hovering
lights and how it maneuvered
several yards behind her.
Ancient Aliens is one of her favorite

shows because she believes we are not alone.
No, we are not, and I am busy going
through forty-eight more books on the Aztecs
and Mayans; the new season has started,
and I must illustrate my progress or
I might get taken straight up in the air.

Picnic

I choked on white sand
at the age of four, my first
family picnic at White Sands
National Monument ten years
after Trinity, Ground Zero twenty
miles from our picnic in the park.
I was blinded by the noon sun
and endless white walls of sand,
the ninety-five-degree heat making me
climb to see the other side.
Distant mountains and a flat
white landscape shimmered and
pushed me away. I rolled down

the dune, laughing and grabbing
fistfuls of sand, the endless glare
bringing tears to my eyes as my
parents watched me from the shade
of the picnic table. I didn't know
the scientists at Los Alamos
made one-dollar bets, wagering on
the explosive yield of the bomb.
I found a quarter under the table and
spent it on a snow cone in El Paso.
"We were told to lie down in the sand,"
scientist Edward Teller explained.

"No one complied. We were
determined to look the beast in the eye."
Picnic laughter and the blindness of
visitors driving on paved roads in
wonder at the endless dunes
and jackrabbits running away,
Robert Oppenheimer staring through

goggles ten thousand yards south of the explosion.
I crying in the back seat of the car on
the drive home, tears running
down my face. I don't recall why I got in
trouble and see my father leaning over
the driver's seat to slap me, my legs pulling
out of the way, white sand raining out
of my pant cuffs into my white tennis shoes.

Miss Atomic Bomb

Arms spread apart, blond curls
bobbing with bright-red lips,
a cotton mushroom cloud on
her white bikini, twenty-one-year-old
Mary Scott is Albuquerque's first
Miss Atomic Bomb, riding on her
atomic float on January 1, 1951,
at the New Year's Day parade.

No paper flower replicas of Fat Man
or Little Boy on the float. It is too
soon after Trinity, so a cardboard
rocket decorates the top of the float
in red, white, and blue. Troops of
Boy Scouts wave as she passes by.
A photo of her straddling the flowery
missile appears in newspapers,

declaring her to be "radiating loveliness
instead of deadly atomic particles."
She is awarded a ten-pound bag of
mushrooms by the Pennsylvania
Mushroom Growers Association.
In her atomic hairdo, Mary helps
serve atomic cocktails at atomic
parties sponsored by the air force.

A drunk mother comes up to her
at one party and stutters, "I took
my daughter to the parade and she
kept yelling that she wanted to grow
up to be an atomic bomb!"
"You mean Miss Atomic Bomb,"
Mary corrected her with a smile.

The mother shrieked, "No!
She wants to be an atomic bomb!"

Mary stares at her before handing
her another drink, the mother's
husband, an army general,
finally dragging her away,
Miss Atomic Bomb visiting military
hospitals for the next year, leaving
colorful paper bombs at the bedside
of each soldier she sees.

Robert Oppenheimer's Chair

*On a photograph of a chair in the
Museum of New Mexico*

When the HUAC committee questioned
Oppenheimer, he refused to give any
names, and they concluded he was
a communist because of his college
friends at Berkeley before the war.

His chair waited for his return to
the desert, where exile is surrounded
by Trinitite, fine green glass created
by the atomic bomb, pieces illegal to collect
now but allowed on jewelry in 1945.

Oppenheimer's chair sits in the middle
of La Jornada del Muerto, the white
desert refusing to reveal its location
because the chair must remain empty
as it glows, its aging yellow wood

painted back then, a chair with
a high back and solid legs not shown
on any map because official betrayal
does not come with a throne.

Still There

The last embrace I gave
my father is still there.

He has been missing
for thirty-seven years.

The last time he whipped
me with his leather belt is

a memory so neutral; the belt
zings through the air.

The last meal my mother
fixed is on the table—

uneaten, steaming hot.
The last time everyone

went to church together
stays in sight of someone

on the cross, bleeding head
bowed, the last monastery

I entered with my mother
still there with a mummified

body of a saint preserved
in glass and waiting for me

under the arch.

The Silence of Federico García Lorca

This is my face. It lies
in the rains of tomorrow.

Seven long birds
cry my eyes.

I am not afraid, because
the orange groves are

clear of serpents.
Sleepwalking women used

to pass here but no longer.
My unborn children track me

down and ask for my voice,
touch my hair.

It is all they can have because
I have seen the grass grow,

and a bee-eating bird
left me bald.

Ask someone else to speak.
I am wrestling with the moon.

Rumins

Hands of doves, palms at rest.
Sweat envisioned in union
with a sack of apples.
Grasses invaded, my voice
anointed with throats in
blue whiskey bottles
delivered by pelicans.
Desire is left after their circling,
leaves whispering echoes before
trees are erased from books
in time for the train to pass.

My scars are never wrong,
love erasing "world" because
"word" is a flute held to my lips—
galaxies wishing they were wrong.
The oranges on the table
have not rolled to the floor,
my fingers turning the clay vase
on the shelf, its blue pattern
of bird-making symbols.

The bay of my notebooks,
the grails of drink, rapture
breaking alleys into smoke,
cedars rising where men
hang family medallions that
make me speak.
The page is quicker than prayer.
Underwater image of earth traded
for the folded flag in hallways

haunted by a child's voice.
I can't pray if the war is on.
The other side is twilight,
this side the past because
the trees drip on archival
paper when I whisper
to the makers,
"Are you ready?
Is there time?"

The Message

The message was delivered
by a small dog, the piece of
paper in its mouth.
I took it and ignored the saliva.

When I opened it, I was
informed that everything was
okay and the world was not
as crazy as I believed.

I sat on the swing on my front
porch and stared at the note.
The world was not a mess.
I had been wrong.

I turned to the dog,
but the thing was gone.
I sat there for a long time
with the note on my hands,

didn't wonder who wrote it,
or how the dog found me.
This happened weeks ago.
I linger at the kitchen table,

drink coffee and think.
I cancel appointments and
sit on the porch, imagine
the forest surrounding my

sanctuary, growing closer.
I sit and stare with the note
in my hand and recall a pair
of little puppy eyes.

Body of Rags / International Bridge between the United States and Mexico

Is it alive? Neither a head, legs nor arms. Torpid against the flange of the supporting girder. An inhuman shapelessness, knees hugged tight up into the self, egg-shaped.

× William Carlos Williams, "Desert Music," 1951, after a visit to El Paso

Yes, I am a body of rags lying
here on the bridge, waiting for

a hot rain to wash me open,
dissolve me off the bridge

because this border is closed.
I rot on the boundary line

and can't enter Juárez,
pennies thrown at me

when a drunk El Pasoan
returns in the darkness

and sees my shape that
makes him hurry across.

No head; decades ago they threw
it in the river without my screams.

My arms were the first to go
when I couldn't climb the wall.

I can never leave this bridge.
I live on the pure line that divides

countries and grabs my hunger
from sliding into Mexico with

my outstretched hands.
I still have my knees.

I used to be sold in Juárez and
smuggled into El Paso, the egg
that floated down the Rio Grande
to break hundreds of miles away

before being thrown back.
I stay on the bridge and can't move.

Do not cross to El Paso without wiping
your shoes of me, one foot on US

concrete, the other scraping away
at my Mexican rags.

When I struggle against the wire fence,
I make sure I salute two flags.

The Dancer

She has about her painted a screen of
pretty doves which flutter their wings.

× William Carlos Williams,
"Desert Music," 1951

The naked dancer extends her arms
in the smoky spotlight, and doves
fly out of her body, disappearing
in the dark cantina, Williams and
his wife staring at her huge breasts,
more birds emerging as she dances
faster, unable to keep up with the beat.

Light glistens off the beaded sequins
around her hips as she reveals to
the Americans what some women
in Juárez do to stay alive, Mexican men
at other tables shouting in a Spanish
Williams can't understand, his Texas
friend bringing him to see a flock of

doves escape the breasts of the dancer,
her nipples shaking in the faces of
the drunks that count birds, Williams
finishing his beer as he hears the flapping
of wings and turns to his wife, who sits
at the table with her eyes closed.

The Alligators

*And those two alligators in the
fountain. There were four. I saw only
two. They were looking right at you all
the time.*

× William Carlos Williams,
"Desert Music," 1951

William Carlos Williams saw two alligators
on his 1951 visit to El Paso, the reptiles

on display in the fountain at San Jacinto
Plaza, the other two disappearing for

one year until I was born in 1952.
He discovered that desert music

is lethal, the alligators suffering
from public abuse, one stabbed with

an arrow, the reptiles finally removed
in the seventies.

The instant I was born, Williams was
gone as the womb drenched me and

made me want to crawl to the cascading
fountain in the square, the creatures

sunning themselves
before diving away.

Playing Poker with Raymond Carver, 1977

He was one of my teachers in El Paso
before he became famous, the university
giving him his first teaching job after
alcoholism destroyed his California marriage.
Few of the writing students knew any
of this, because only a handful of us were
invited to his tiny apartment to play
poker after our weekly workshop.

We arrived promptly after class,
his place near campus messy with
dozens of empty Pepsi bottles
everywhere, ashtrays holding mounds
of cigarette butts, Ray smoking
and filling himself with sodas to
keep from drinking again, the card
games not as important as hanging
out with a writer we knew was going
to take some of us somewhere.

He said to simply write our poems
and stories and get out of the way,
his style of saying it making me sit
back and watch the others play
because I was not good at poker,
Ray turning to me with thick
eyebrows and asking, "Did you quit?"
I sat up and quickly got back into
the game and didn't know what move
to make because many things were
shared through the cigarette
smoke and weekly gatherings
where our futures were decided by
drawing aces and spades.

Homage to the Father

After abandoning us
for forty epic years,

we suffer your death
like a slow dance,

my sisters, your daughters
wrinkled and old before

I can get there,
my brown skin scratching

at my heaving breast,
a thing that generates

new ways of weeping
without leaving a trace

or admitting we are
no longer afraid.

Last Night

Last night the bees came, the tops
of the barrel cactus split open
by the heat, bees darting into the night
to find the place they belonged.
I heard them in the canyon and waited
in the broken trunk of the cottonwood,
hiding in there to learn how swarms
of bees teach men in their sleep,
so the sweet desert is no longer
the honey that sticks to my lips
and opens the dirt road until I find
the slashed barrels and take a drink.

Last night the bats invented aromas,
followed their black flight out of Carlsbad
Caverns to feed on peyote plants around
the entrance, this documented myth
broken when I reached the opening in
the earth and saw the blue lights,
headed back to my car without visiting
because I approached the wrong cave,
smelled the smoke, bats brushing my head
with the magnet of guano that forced
me to leave without entering the ground.

Last night a mountain lion entered
the town and was trapped in a car wash,
police shooting it and not giving it a chance,
the streets marked with the claws of the old,
my hands slapping walls and leaving a mark,
a distant buzz mistaken for light poles
blinking across the city, the clay jars on
my porch brimming with water where
bees hover until I go into the great
fields of cactus, directing the river to
follow me without flooding the earth.

La Frontera

Someone found the writings of the madman.
In his text, you are standing under the trees.

A mighty figure is seated there, covered in leaves.
He waits there without speaking because

his language will be crushed by cathedrals.
Hernán Cortés had twenty-nine horses killed by the Aztecs.

On the other side of the house
where you grew up, they uncovered

an ancient burial site and built a freeway.
Enter quietly because white hair is outlawed.

The Lone Ranger is the earliest image
you recall of childhood television.

There is also religion, a canister, and
an only child crying in the street.

When Basho stood at the gates of
the emperor, two frogs leaped out

of his robe and entered first.
The narrative of immigration control

integrates and alienates, the magnolia
turning yellow as autumn rests in

the branches that shade the closed book,
its cover open to paradise, the shadow

of the leaf-covered figure fertilizing
the magnolia before it was time to grieve.

On the other side of the bridge you crossed
was a child with no legs, begging for coins.

The sky is constellated by voyages like this.
When you arrived at the last church

you ever entered, everyone was kneeling,
and no one looked up.

Midnight Rider

I was wearing my Duane Allman T-shirt
when I heard Gregg died. I wonder
what I wore the day Duane was killed in

a motorcycle crash forty-six years ago and three
weeks after I saw the Allman Brothers in
concert in Las Cruces, New Mexico.

My best friend Bill and I were near
the front row, close to our favorite band.
We lived one of rock 'n' roll's clichés—

rock bands form bonds of brotherhood
among musicians and their fans, rising
from our fanatic souls, air guitars and

stoned afternoons in the desert playing
"Whipping Post" over and over, rock
clichés originating in memories of our

days as drooling fans.
I listened to Gregg's voice through decades
because Allman brotherhood included

the disappearance of alcoholic Bill.
I have not been able to find him in El Paso
after twenty years of searching.

The last time I saw him, he told me he got
rid of his albums because his stereo was stolen,
but he had the Allman's music in his head and

sang the songs to himself whenever he wanted.
When I played Gregg's music on May 27,
it was for Bill and our twin guitars burning on

the road between Las Cruces and El Paso,
Gregg's defiant voice reassuring me that we
will rise again, somewhere in the desert, to play.

The Allman Brothers will take the stage
because Gregg's songs connect highways
from teenage concerts to an old man at home

pausing his stereo because the pair of doves
he spotted on his backyard fence have returned
and are cooing as he listens at the window.

River

If I gave away my country,
there would be affection in the cities.

If I stumbled upon flags in the canyons, women
in labor would demand their sons return.

If I complied, I would be led to the fountain
where Emilio Zapata drank before his death.

If I wore the sombrero of stereotype, I would hide
inside the ovens where no one baked bread.

If I caught smoke from the mountain, animals
would become extinct and never find their way.

If I knew the difference between knowing
and having, I would take one word to find

the wound of release,
my books dissolving to the touch.

If I convinced you my habits were things
to come, you would reward me with guitars

on street corners where intensive care is
spray-painted on the bricks.

If I gave away my country, there would be
flesh in the cities.

If I released my rivals to consume the playgrounds,
they would pockmark the chairs of their fathers with

sweat poured from things they could never say.
If I waited to say them myself, my dogs would seize

their prey and never obey me again.
If I cut open a head of lettuce to find the worm,

the fields would no longer let me stand.
If I came home to grow my hair, I would be

the first bald son to make it back.
If I stopped to acknowledge the impaled

snake on the fence, no one would believe me,
only say, "Enough is enough," and lead me

to a waiting truck full of desperate men.

Part Three

The Poem of One Hundred Tongues

The poem of one hundred tongues realigns the saxophone
until two hundred eardrums respond,

the music building into a text that wants to spill
the wine out of the conches.

The poem of one hundred tongues tattoos many faces,
the images showing mouths are outlawed.

The poem hides those faces until they open
like cactus flowers stepped on by bare feet.

The poem of one hundred tongues paints ninety-eight faces brown,
leaving two in the sun of white, words forming

in the twins—one for truth and one for lying.
When fifty throats stop writing, the sound of dying

is mistaken for the first word.
When the other fifty throats keep writing,

light embraces everything, the sound of living
mistaken for the last word.

The poem of one hundred tongues fills the baskets at dawn,
demands a prayer to touch one hundred wet foreheads,

beads of sweat drying into moles on the skin mistaken
for periods at the end of one hundred sentences.

Snap

Let other people speak for you.
Their foreheads are as sweaty as yours.
Close the white door because
the world is about to snap.
Let the dictator smell your feet.
You have been running for sixty-eight years,
and your heels are sore.
When the dictator snorts
the pandemic will arrive,
and he will snap.

Let others pray for you.
Their faith is not lost
in the dusty desert wind.
Their practice of genuflection
makes their knees snap
on the benches of sin.
When they ask you for favors,
do not make a sound.
Time is present in the dust
inside the candleholders where
someone found the ashes
of your notes.

Let others speak because
silence comes from a mother's
hands after she snapped at
you because she insisted men
were digging a tunnel under
her house.
It is not the way to get home,
because the unadorned Mexican
trees prefer the fighting rooster

with its bleeding claws, razors
strapped to its legs so it can
slash to the center of the light
where there is a revolution no
one acts on, buckets of blood
cleansing the color of the roses
raining down in the churchyard.

Meditation Near Hatch, New Mexico

A fire develops
above the sun,

flames hitting the river
and opening

the violent world
toward its ignorance.

x

When you left
the desert,

your teacher
stayed behind.

The old poet
hiked alone and

dropped dead
on his daily walk.

It took his family
three days to find him.

By then, his spirit
had left the canyons,

his body waiting for
the next poem to

rise from the dust
and keep walking.

x

The thick salt cedars pause on the bank
as the mud blesses me with brown feet,

a blue egg floating by in the current,
the mighty bend in the Rio Grande

a magnetic rope of water where I have
stopped, the last time bringing two coyotes

out of the reeds, thirsty stares and sharp
ears breaking sunlight into worries

I couldn't reach near the tallest cottonwood
where they disappeared.

x

I am surprised an old
out-of-print book,

along with a friend, both
mention Kilbourn Hole

a few days apart.
The volcanic crater, forty miles

west of El Paso, looks like an
enormous burned footprint

sinking into the earth.
The last time I went there,

forty-two years ago, the hole spread
its black rocks across a wild

landscape of snake dens,
tarantulas, and millions of

pieces of blue glass.
When I collected a handful,

the pieces shined beyond
the riches of ash that were

piled to the sky,
the hike to the bottom

extinguishing light,
a deep step into blackness

I did not recognize without
rock faces asking, in peace,

how old I had become.

x

All I remember from childhood is
the bright stinging sun heating

my head until I couldn't breathe—
the scorching light forcing me

outside in the 114 degree summer
so I could grow blind and try to

blink and push everything away,
the white revolving flash of noon

sun covering what I thought and
believed as the sweat poured down

my face and I shut my watering eyes.
When I opened them, the punishing

sun did not yield until late evening,
when all was burned.

☓

Yesterday, I came across the word
sunbeam twice in my daily readings

and realized it was a rare image, two
different writers using it as a light

that prefers to hide in the oaks,
the ocotillos, and those endless salt

cedars refusing to drown my need
to stand here and be blinded by

what the current took.

Table and Lamp

Zbigniew Herbert wrote of
an elephant that fell in love

with a hummingbird.
I saw the tiny thing as it flashed

beyond the cherry tree
and flew into the past.

My dream greets a friend
who refuses to stand

near the border wall.
Each sorrow I share is blessed

by resembling his sorrow.
Why do whiskers grow

faster on old men with desires?
I want to sing of mercy, too.

Fat Saint

Fat Saint off a calendar photo on the wall,
why do you make me shudder?
Fat Saint with a brown face even my
grandmother would not kiss, though
she bowed and prayed to your light.
So what if I am afraid?
The hardest *susto* is the fear of capturing
my own shadow, placing it in the flower-
pot and watching it grow.

Fat Saint burned in the Inquisition,
your tortured feet were branded under
the sign of a god who forgave you long ago.
Fat Saint who haunts the barrio with a wicked
wand, a broom, and starving dogs at your feet.
When you hear the chants, don't fall off the wall.
When the Spanish conquered Mexico City,

sacrificed hearts were cut out by the Aztecs.
They didn't know the emptiness in the chest
is the *susto* of the ancestors who had nothing
to do with the history of conquest, worked in
the fields as illiterate *campesinos* dying on
the roads north toward El Paso.
So what if I still have nightmares?
Who cares if the voice in my sleeping throat
never matches how I talk each day?

Fat Saint, your calendar photo is fading, and
your face is more familiar with every death.
Men and women in dirty clothes unroll their beds,
stare at me as if they know something frightens me
and gives me reasons for the language of embraces.
Fat Saint, if I could peel your photo off the wall
without leaving a silhouette of the spot
you never blessed, I would.

No One Moved

There was a steeple, and
a light existed.
Walls were strong and painted
with hallways leading nowhere.

Men rose and fell.
Long hair grew down their backs.
Women fed, and women were granted.
Roses grew, and roses left thorns.
Windows opened and never closed.
Damaged spines spit out hallucinations.
There were clay bodies everywhere.

No one moved.
Knees were bent in the circle of rock.
They were able to imagine fire.
The clay bowl discovered itself,
and carnal scenes were emblazoned.
A flight of roots became a cough,
and they listened.

Clay hands built the text.
Cracks in the sun and the brick.
There are ruins at rest.
Dig there because the body
that opens its hands first will
extend the lifelines on its palms.

Ears Full of Thorns

The music of silence was composed
when Santa Fe fell in 1619,
Pueblo people cutting off
the heads of the Spaniards.
My mother denied a slap on
her face, turned the other cheek
like Christ, and asked for
it again.

The angels who guided
the conquistador betrayed him
and left him to die in the canyon.
The wolf believed in rosaries,
chewed a bundle of them
before he was shot in
the season of faults.

My brother never woke from
the umbilical cord around his neck.
The music of loss and defeat
is the beauty composed during
the shattering of the clay ovens.

My streets were lined in brown
when mud was legal and no one
felt they had to put iron bars
in every window.
Waiting for the signal to attack,
Juan Carlos Arrete entered heaven
by welcoming the spear that
inflated his body and set him on
the black horse he rode as a boy.

There is no mercy when
the rat leaves the hole and
a Gila Monster emerges,
its black body dotted in pink,
its ugly head flashing its tongue
to see if the blood of
our waiting has dried.
What binds us is a passageway
to the jars of salt where
my grandmother diminished
our history by chanting to
the coyote mounted on the wall.

The notes of darkness and
headaches are the song of
a passing truck full of
migrant workers on the way
to slow deaths, the fields
of cotton and chile destroyed
by the black fumes that
took over the valley.
The mouth of judgment
is a shoeless foot.

When Cochise erased
the markings on the rocks,
twenty-eight of his warriors
were killed by the Mexicans.
When Emiliano Zapata was gunned
down in conspiracy, three white
stallions were set free in
the town square by his enemies.
When André Breton found
a plate of blue feathers by
his cot in the Zuni pueblo,
he wrote seven poems and

crossed the desert on foot.
When a tiny lizard was eaten
by the schoolboy on a dare,
his friends stared at him
and walked away for good.

The ear bristles with love,
but no one listens to the choir,
because the moment of bowing
down is covered in purple
curtains thrown on the bodies.
My turn consists of taking a twig,
tying a blade of grass around it,
then holding the twig in the air
for a falcon to take.

My father had a blue panther
tattooed on his body when
he was in the navy.
My father cut the panther
off his shoulder, scraping
the skin raw until his past
was erased and he did not
have to share it with anyone.

When smoke was interpreted
as a distant signal,
the dancers arrived.
When smoke slashed
the eyes red, the chosen danced.
When smoke was an alphabet
floating across the desert,
the town was founded.
When smoke took
the panther from my father's
body, I watched in silence.

Ten below Zero, Country Road, Northfield, Minnesota

There is old ecstasy under the great snowfields.
Their black trees belong to the story of
returning without punishment for worshipping
the rhythm of the storm that captures desire

as it blinds the sun and finds the prayers
embedded in the ice, the curving road
sending those whispers to the table left
inside the empty house in the distance.

We freeze in a profile that allows for grace
and white drifts where the falling temperature
demands we believe in the rare visit from
the white crow, the white buffalo, and ghosts

that stagger in the blizzard to find there is
one kind of sleep in the cracked ice.

Three Snowy Owls

Deep winter and a rare migration
of snowy owls in Minnesota
passes through our cul-de-sac,
neighbors saying three of them
are in the trees each night, one
of them sparing their dog when
they accidentally let it out, white
shapes appearing then vanishing

as the hooting finally entered
my house, the call making us rise
at three in the morning, the steady
cry the loudest I have heard
from a bird of prey, backyard
darkness suddenly splitting open
as my wife at the window sees
the owl spring heavily off the oak

and fly over the house, leaving us
to wonder what we were told in
our sleep, why the owl filled
the air, repeating itself in isolated
rhythm that penetrated every
room of my cold fear and an
unclaimed longing it ignored,
its changing white form stealing

the moment where we started
to understand it had to be what
we could never dream.

A few nights later, I heard it
alone and did not wake my wife
while the owl hooted for one
hour, its sound taking the night
to a ten-below silence where
the bird kept answering
my lonely greed.

El Paso Massacre, August 3, 2019

I was born in El Paso in 1952
at Southwest General Hospital,
the original old building torn down
decades ago, a new hospital built
on the same site and now reported
to be one of the most haunted
buildings in El Paso, ghosts
and spirits seen there often.

×

Some of the first images on television
show people running out of the Walmart,
running toward the river nearby,
people running to the border a common sight.

×

The shooter's manifesto was reported
to use some of the same phrases as
Trump's speeches.

×

Between the end of the Civil War in 1865,
and 1930, rough estimates claim at least
five thousand Mexicans shot or lynched by
Texas Rangers throughout the state.

×

In El Paso, the last record store
I shopped at before moving away in 1978
used to be next to the Walmart.
At that time, black metal, heavy metal,
and death metal were big—El Paso's
answer to punk, which never took off there.

×

They interviewed a Mexican grandmother
and grandfather who were shot in the store,
both alive and in the hospital, their grandchildren
surrounding their beds and reminding me that
El Paso was always a town of grandparents.

×

In 1519 Juan de Oñate crossed El Paso del Norte
on horseback, leading his conquistadors north,
several horses drowning in the river, three of
the Spanish solders never returning from
the first expedition through the desert.

×

The shooter told police he came to town
to "kill as many Mexicans" as he could.
Killing Mexicans was almost a high school
cry among the football players who called me
"beaner," "dumb Mexican," "Spic," "greaser," and "Chuy."

×

An off-duty soldier, stationed at Fort Bliss
in El Paso, saved the lives of several children
by leading them out of the Walmart,
even pulling out his personal Glock,
conceal and carry laws alive and well
in the state. Besides the cops, where was
everybody with their guns?

×

The Texas Governor said
the mass shooting
was not "like Texas."
Texas leads the nation in
mass killings each year.

✗

On CNN, a young protester
holds up a sign.
"If I Die in a Mass Killing,
Drop my Body at the White House."

✗

My sister's house is three miles
from the Walmart where she and
my brother-in-law shop every Saturday.
He was playing golf that day in
the one-hundred-degree heat, so they didn't go.

✗

Shrines, flowers, white crosses from
a Chicago man who devotes his life
to making wooden crosses for mass-
killing victims all over the country,
telling CNN that he has made hundreds
since he started years ago.

✗

The Texas War Cry will be changed from
"Remember the Alamo" to
"Remember the Walmart."

✗

The brown waters of the Rio Grande
keep flowing nearby.

First Anniversary, El Paso Massacre

They lie dead
but not forgotten,

the hot desert sun
reaching 109 as

each body stirs
on its way to

a galaxy that
welcomes them

as burning stars,
imploding light,

constellations
whispering across

the heavens,
"There is no blood here."

"What a Man Wants Is the Power to Name the Terms of His Rescue"

× Stephen Dunn,
"What Men Want," 2009

If I had that power,
I would have rescued
myself long ago, and
my private landscape would
remain mountain and sky.
These are terms I can accept,
not tell anyone I am growing
stronger each day, the dirt trail
never leading where it should,
people vanishing from our lives
so we can steal their power.

If I had that power,
I would measure how
much strength I stole from
my father who just died
without saying a word to me.
He was learning to rescue himself,
because the most beautiful thing
I can recall are my working father's
worn shoes at the foot of his bed.
That beauty reflects in the sentence
I wrote with my Parkinson's hand,
not on the page but in punishment—
a sentence for the power of rescue,
a silent manner of living without shame.

The Bend at the Rio Grande

The sun's brilliance reveals
the river will outlast your

lifting hands if you stand
near the great turn of water

near Hatch, New Mexico,
and follow the current that

is aware of how you live,
the river never changing

course because the light
rises inside the sudden

flight of two blue herons
above the bend.

ACKNOWLEDGMENTS

Thanks to the editors of the following publications where some of these poems first appeared, sometimes in slightly different form:

Bitter Oleander: "Ears Full of Thorns"

Caliban: "The Silence of Fernando Pessoa," "Serpent Words," "Pueblo Dancers, Santo Domingo, New Mexico, 2004," "The Silence of Aime Cesaire," and "The Dancer."

Fifth Wednesday Journal: "Solar Eclipse Totality, 2017," "Quietly Look Back," and "Picnic"

Pleides: "El Paso Massacre, August 3, 2019"

Plume: "'What a Man Wants Is the Power to Name the Terms of His Rescue'"

Poetry: "Body of Rags / International Bridge between the United States and Mexico"

The following poems appeared in *Some Holy Ghost*, a chapbook published by Mesilla Press in 2018:

"Two Hands at San Elizario"

"Suggest Paradise"

"T-shirt Shop on Santa Fe Street"

"Solar Eclipse Totality, 2017"

"The Silence of Aime Cesaire"

"The Silence of Fernando Pessoa"

The following poem appeared in *Rumins*, a chapbook published by Miel Press in 2016:

"Photographs of the Dead"